Frozen by Fire

Frozen by Fire

A Documentary in Verse

of the Triangle Factory Fire of 1911

Donald Kentop

Most of the poems in this work were published under the same title in a limited edition. For the Black Heron Press edition, new material has been included.

ISBN: 978-1-936364-39-8
Library of Congress control number 2014911753

Cover art: Nina O'Neill
Book design: Jan Nicosia
Cover photograph: Lewis Hine, The Granger Collection

Manufactured in the United States

Black Heron Press
Post Office Box 614
Anacortes, Washington 98221
www.blackheronpress.com

To the victims and survivors,
and to Anna Rosen, survivor,
killed at home by fire later that year.

My heart rouses
   thinking to bring you news
     of something

that concerns you

from "Asphodel, That Greeny Flower,"
   William Carlos Williams

Contents

Illustrations

Introduction

Since the Triangle Shirtwaist Factory fire in 1911, thousands of New Yorker University students have attended classes in the Brown Building unaware that it was once called the Asch Building and was the site of a tragic fire that ravaged the very space they occupied as students. I was one of those students.

Decades later, after realizing what had happened there, I wrote the poem, "The Brown Building." In researching the poem, I was moved by the survivors' accounts of their ordeal and the extraordinary character and resilience they displayed in telling their stories. I began to writre about them as well, then realized the poems needed the context of the times, and so abandoned myself to an entire project. However, the survivors' accounts remain at the core of the work. In the course of writing the book, I have grown attached to them, both as young people who survived and as old people who were asked to remember what happened.

The story spans more than one hundred years, beginning with abysmal working conditions, the fire itself, how it shocked the nation, led to historic labor and safety legislation, and then was largely forgotten for decades. Not until the commemoration of its fiftieth anniversary did the tragedy begin to reassert itself in the public's consciousness and were the survivors' stories retold and recorded.

Now, after its centennial, the story is still shocking, and relevant to working people, unions, women, immigrants, minorities, teenage youth—to all who want to preserve the gains made since the fire, and to protect them from erosion and assault. Elsewhere, the year may as well be 1911 as people continue to be killed in staggering numbers on the job, and many others put at needless risk under the same preventable circumstances.

This history, drawn from a variety of primary sources, is not exhaustive but is rich in detail, and lends itself to the density, economy, and impact of verse. It was a challenge to balance dates, numbers, and proper nouns in the work with metric faithfulness. Just as the book claims historical faithfulness rather than historical perfection, so does the versification. Yet, the restrictions of verse, paradoxically, liberate characters and events from the prosaics of reportage and open a way of learning through the heart.

Leon Stein, author of The Triangle Fire, *gazing from a window of the Brown Building, ca. 1960.*

Kheel Center, Cornell University

Frozen by Fire

...in the world that He created as He willed

Rage and wail, collapse and let the world
see how we grieve in Białystok and mourn
in Sicily; how we rip the hateful
shirtwaists from our backs and rend the voile,
tucked batiste, and horrid high-stand collars;
how we tear the flat felled seams and plackets;
pull our hair and dress in black, wear sackcloth,
dust our heads, seated low on boxes,
ashamed to be alive, frozen by fire.
We lift our hands to heaven and we call,
and wait for God to answer. How can we
defend Him in the face of such injustice?
We cannot, and so we kneel and pray
the *De Profundis*, and rise for the *Kaddish*.

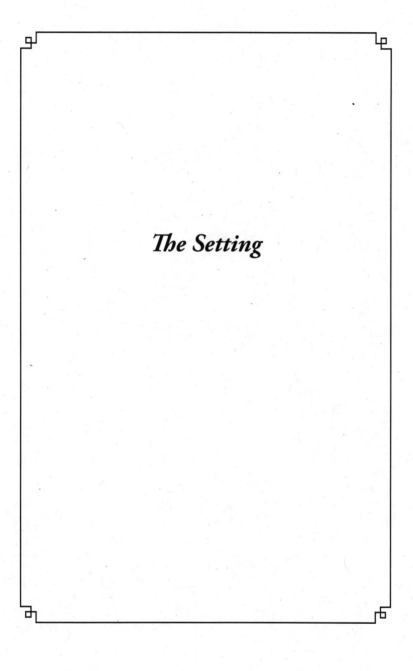

The Setting

The Brown Building

We smoked cigarettes at NYU
and talked of Eisenhower, Kerouac,
the Beats. Before rock 'n' roll we puffed
on Camels, flicked our ashes on the floor,
and rode elevators to our classrooms
in what had once been called the Asch Building.

We did not know. There were no markers left
behind to even whisper of the fire
of 1911. Today, three are mounted
on the corner. Cast from molten bronze,
they tell the story, yet are placed too high
to run your fingers on the frozen words.

In different times, instead of sewing shirts,
Molly Gerstein might have sat beside us
during freshman English; Ida Brodsky,
a sleeve setter—or a science major?—
and Jacob Klein might have been a friend.
Kate Leone was too young for college.

The Triangle Shirtwaist Factory sewed
the high-necked blouses worn by Gibson Girls.
The shop took up the top three floors, the eighth,
the ninth, and tenth, which were consumed by flames
one Saturday in March at quitting time.
The holocaust still radiates today.

One hundred and forty-six immigrant men
and women burned or jumped to deaths. Some leapt
in twos and threes while holding hands, their skirts
on fire, from the same window spaces
we looked through for spring in Greenwich Village,
impatient for McSorley's nickel ale.

An X in Red

Let Gettysburg and Shiloh sprawl at ease.
We pray they never feel again the tread
of boots on earth where fallen soldiers bled,

yet no amount of grass or malls or trees
or parking lots, not even if the seas
invade, can time obliterate the dead's

coordinates, forever fixed in place.
The sidewalks in New York have been repaved,
the building where the workers slaved

is since renamed, remodeled, but its face
and masonry the same, still holds the space
that burned and windows where the dying waved.

The plaques, neglected prophets, mutely plead
their tale to those who hurry blindly straight
ahead, the city dweller running late,

and should the accidental tourist read
the words, they seldom feel the need
to crane their necks or take the time to wait

or lift their feet and look beneath their shoes
to find the X in red, the faded blot
where once a seamstress died. The story shot

around the world. The nation, bruised,
awakened, yet bodies fall and pile fused
against locked doors, and X still marks the spot.

A Matter of Time

In Newark, when a garment factory burned
and twenty-six young girls and women died
four months before the Greenwich Village fire,
New York City's fire chief had warned,
"It's a matter of time before it happens here"
and then the story faded from the news.

The Newark inquest found no one to blame,
not the owner, nor the tenant, nor public
official, nor had any laws been broken.
It was accepted, bad things simply happened.
The country tolerated accidents
that claimed one hundred workers' lives a day.

The New York City Code was clear and called
for two-hundred and fifty feet of space
per worker, but the Asch Building's ceilings
were high. The law let bosses count the space
above the workers' heads. They jammed them in,
by the letter, not the spirit of the law.

The cutters felt they were elite and smoked
despite the posted signs. The floors were oily,
the scrap bins overflowed, machines were set
too close, the aisles were narrow, doors were locked
or opened inward, the fire escape was flimsy
and the building, built one stairway short,

so fragile, trembling for the one mistake.
A few days later, when the shop had cooled,
the floors and walls seemed ready to be scrubbed,
repainted, and reoccupied. The Asch
Building was in fact built fireproof,
and yet the people working there were not.

The Shirtwaist Kings, Max Blanck (left) and Isaac Harris.

Kheel Center, Cornell University

1911

In England, the Edwardians were poised
upon the peak of power, while the French
reveled gaily in La Belle Époque,
and in America, a hangover
from the Gilded Age, when Irving Berlin
composed "Alexander's Ragtime Band,"

Scott Joplin published *Treemonisha*, Gustav
Mahler led the New York Philharmonic,
Caruso sang at the Met, and Ty Cobb hit
four-twenty, and more immigrants arrived.
Boatloads from the south and east of Europe
sailed west searching for their golden dream.

They made the Lower Eastside the most densely
populated area on earth,
worse than Bombay, according to Rudyard Kipling.
Broome Street, Mott Street, Hester and Canal Street
were overwhelmed with buzzing hives of people,
bursting-ripe with possibility.

The myth proclaimed the cobblestones were made
of gold, but they were merely gilded; gold
so thin it covered up the earth. Beneath
were people on whose shoulders wealth depended,
a wealth beyond belief, and owned by less
than one percent of people in America.

This was the time of the Triangle fire:
exploding riches, strikes and modern art,
emerging science, muckrakers, ragtime,
privilege challenged, looming war, the spread
of phones and cars, aeroplanes, a woman's
right to vote, the RMS *Titanic* launched.

The Shirtwaist Kings

As far as sweatshops went, the Triangle
was said to be the best, unsafe, noisy,
overcrowded, strict, with grueling quotas,
but also light and airy. After half
a year of strikes the pay was fair, but still
they had no union and no safety rules.

The owners, Russian immigrants made good,
were Isaac Harris and Max Blanck. The two
worked hard, did a million a year, bought Cadillacs
and Packards, and luxury homes on the Upper Westside.
Despite their wealth they lay awake at night
and fretted over pilfered shirts and lace,

and so they locked the doors, had purses searched.
Even Joseph Flecher, loyal lackey
and bookkeeper, said money used for bribes
and entertaining customers appeared
to have no limit, yet regarding wages
they "were stingy and you couldn't get a raise."

Isaac Harris

Flecher said that "Harris had a quiet
nature, a serious man, tight and highly
inclined for female pleasure, highly. Short
and strict, he knew the factory, dealt with workers.
He never smiled, but would stop a girl
and say, *I'll see you after office hours.*

He looked forward to meeting nice girls."
He also had a sneaky habit where
he rifled through coat pockets in the dressing
room to search for union dues receipts.
After the fire broke out, even then,
someone reportedly kept searching purses.

Max Blanck

Blanck was beefy, taller than Harris,
and when they stood together, both in derbies,
their photograph suggests Laurel and Hardy.
But there the likeness ends; they both were smart,
both hotly anti-union, mean enough
to hire thugs to break the picket lines.

Blanck was more a schmoozer, the outside man,
a diplomat, and said to be a bit
more human. His job was to bring in business,
he didn't deal with workers. His concern,
the customer, while Harris knew all there was
to know about the making of a shirt.

Sketch by Charles Dana Gibson

The Gibson Girl

The images that flowed from Charles Gibson's
pen were icons of femininity
and drawn for the Gilded Age. Her face
was circulated coast-to-coast in print,
on every magazine, every product
to which her loveliness could be attached.

Also famous for her wit and spirit,
she defined her sex and generation.
With ample hips and bosom, she was tall
and dignified, her waist absurdly pinched
by busk and corset, and her bouffant hair
was piled high above a slender neck.

She was traditional, yet self-possessed,
had charm and spunk, was single but remote
and inaccessible, called mischievous,
a tease, and with her smitten men portrayed
as bumbling. She dressed smartly, favoring
a simple shoe-length skirt and crisp, white "waist."

She bought shirtwaists by the millions, mass
produced relentlessly by her sisters
in New York sweatshops. None so ruthless or
efficient as the Triangle shop,
whose prodded operators stiffened, bent
at their machines to satisfy demand.

Mary Leventhal was twenty-two,
American born, popular and smart,
with aspirations, wit, a sense of fashion;
she too had bouffant hair, and was burned
so badly her dentist identified her body.
She likely wore a Blanck and Harris shirtwaist.

Bupkis

The fallow ground of the poor would yield
much fruit, but injustice sweeps it away.

Proverbs 13:23

The garment business was a contract business.
A jobber took a job, his workers sewed
in dark and dirty unsafe tenements
and lofts. He paid them *bupkis* for their sweat.
On roiling Hester Street, the "Pig Market"
was always there with cheap replacement cogs.

When people served as slaves they were counted
on the books as assets, but a garment
worker's value lay in what she sewed
today. Accept subsistence pay or quit,
feel free to find another job, a form
of freedom made expressly for the rich.

One owner, pressed about the fire hazards
in his shop, snarled "Let them burn, they're cattle
anyway." He spoke what others thought:
they weren't very bright, they'll rob you blind,
so keep your wages low, it's common sense,
and fires—just a cost of doing business.

The Triangle used "inside" contractors,
who in turn would pay a team to sew.
The company did not employ the workers,
thus kept their distance, but contractors
also sewed, and when they paid their team,
often had little left to pay themselves.

Security meant keep your head down, sew
like hell, and never mind the needle through
your finger, or the thread they charged you for,
or new hires who would work for nothing,
yet they supported families, they saved
for steamship tickets, and they scrimped for plays.

bupkis: beans

Clara Lemlich

Her fiery speech at a meeting of the Women's Trade Union League sparked the "Uprising of the Twenty Thousand."

Kheel Center, Cornell University

The Uprising of the Twenty Thousand, 1909

Young Jacob Klein was dark eyed, handsome, gentle,
and worked directly for Harris and Blanck.
A contractor, Jacob counted his pay
and figured, after paying operators,
there was little left for him to live on.
He shouted in the shop that he was sick

of being driven like a slave and called
for better pay in front of everyone.
They heard, including factory manager
Samuel Bernstein, related to the owners.
He was short but powerful and feared,
and ordered Klein to leave. When Klein refused,

Bernstein dragged him out the door and slapped
him as he went. He broke Jacob's glasses
and tore his shirt. A walkout followed soon but fizzled.
In 1909, the Women's Trade Union
League called New York City's largest strike.
Locked out, the Triangle workers joined.

Petite Clara Lemlich, an activist,
was badly beaten by one Charley Rose,
a gangster; Ben Sklaver, by Johnny Spanish,
another hoodlum. Hired prostitutes
and pimps attacked the pickets with fists and claws
and hat pins while the police stood by.

The Triangle workers won their raises
and shorter hours, but they failed to form
a union or to change the safety rules.
The movement that made labor history sprang
from the courage of thousands of immigrant girls.
Half of the Triangle's dead were still in their teens.

A strike "newsie," selling papers like Sylvia Riegler did.

Kheel Center, Cornell University

Dora Maisler

The judge said, "Dora, are you here again?"
because during the strike they arrested us
so often they called us by our first names.
The bosses hired prostitutes to beat
the girls, but when the cutters, who were men,
were on the picket lines, they hired hoodlums.

When they attacked us, we fought back, but we
would be the only ones the police arrested.
It was a regular Korean War.
That was when I had my teeth knocked out
and I was hauled to court at Jefferson Market.
Some judges felt so strong against the strike

that girls were tried and sentenced to the workhouse.
The first night at the Tombs, and then five days
hard labor in the jail on Blackwell's Island.
The place was like its name, but only worse.
Twenty-five weeks later we won higher
wages, shorter hours, but—no union.

The day of the fire, after work, I planned
to go to Jacob's Moving Picture Theater,
and so I bought a brand new suit
and was changing when I saw the flames.
I ran to the elevator, skirt
in hand. I squeezed in and the cable broke.

Out on the street, my clothes were torn, I was
naked and freezing when a nice man gave
his overcoat to me and took me home.
You want to hear a good one? I'm in my bed,
exhausted, and a fire starts next door.
I said, "I guess it's time for me to go."

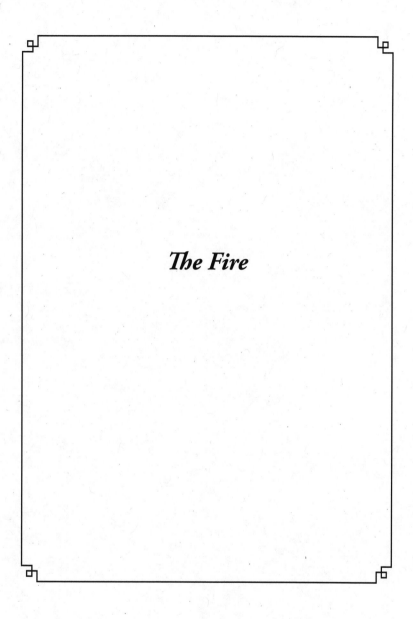

The Fire

First Fall

A chic Fifth Avenue address began
at Washington Square and ran north, uptown.
Due south, Fifth changed to Thompson Street with lines
of tenements that rose like canyon walls.
Between the ghetto and the silk top hats,
the park, a commons with a marble arch.

With winter's grip relaxed, the people strolled
its paths to breathe the mild afternoon.
The social classes, keeping to themselves,
mainly orbited each other, never
touched, except to buy an ice cream treat
or to get a shoeshine for a nickel.

Late afternoon, that Saturday in March,
the Asch Building's gray facade appeared
serene. A half-block from the park, it served
as backdrop for the urban scene except
for five hundred invisible girls inside
whose terrible ordeal was underway.

The first public sign of trouble was
a "big puff" blowing out an eighth-floor window
followed by the sound of breaking glass.
Below, a horse panicked at the noise,
whinnied, bolted and, wild-eyed, careened
down the cobblestones, chased by its driver.

A man yelled, "Look, someone's there, all right...
throwing out his best goods." The bundle opened.
Before he grasped the truth, the girl was dead.
The frantic phone calls and the fire box
alarm were both turned in at four-forty,
about the time the girls began to jump.

The only fire escape collapsed, killing more than twenty people.

Kheel Center, Cornell University

Sylvia Riegler Kimeldorf

We came here from Romania. I went
to work in the garment industry
when I was just sixteen and soon I found
myself in the middle of the big
shirtwaist-makers strike of 1909,
"The Uprising of the Twenty Thousand."

It was the coldest winter in twenty years.
I froze, hawking papers on the sidewalk
to raise a little money for the strike.
Pickets were arrested every day.
One magistrate, his name was Olmstead, said
to join a strike was offensive to God.

I managed to escape the fire when
a girlfriend dragged me toward the windows, but
my feeling said it was the wrong direction.
I took the stairway on the Greene Street side.
Leo Brown unlocked the door, then fought
the girls, because the door opened inward.

My intuition and my fear of heights
saved me, but my girlfriend jumped. They took
me to a Chinese import house across
the street, and gave me milk to calm me down.
Through the window I could see bodies
fall and hit the sidewalk with a bounce.

First Response

I learned a new sound…It was the thud
of a speeding, living body on a stone sidewalk.

William Gunn Shepherd,
Milwuakee Journal, March 27, 1911

The smoke and muffled blast had drawn a crowd
which then pulled back as bodies plummeted
and struck the sidewalk. Fire whistles could
be heard approaching. On mounted patrol in the park,
Officer James Meehan, the first responder,
spurred his horse and galloped to the scene.

He entered the building and ran up the stairs two steps
at a time and heard the sound of workers pounding
in panic behind a locked door. They'd stumbled down
the fire escape moments before it collapsed
and reentered through a sixth-floor window.
Meehan kicked in the door and led the group

down the spiral staircase out to the street.
The first officers to reach the scene
were from the Mercer Street Station House;
perhaps among them those who used their clubs
against these girls, the same who struck the year
before. Later, they lowered and tagged their bodies.

The workers at the windows waved their arms,
ready to jump, alive and sound as those
below who shouted, "Don't jump. Here they come,
stay there." As the fire wagons' sirens
came closer, they were forced to jump and struck
the sidewalk with an awful sound.

Around the corner, people were on fire.
They jammed the windows as they fought to die
by falling than by flame. The jam gave way,
the human torches tumbled awkwardly,
bodies on flaming bodies, as firemen
played their hoses on the burning mound.

The spray of the fire hoses was merely a mist by the time it reached the top three floors.

Kheel Center, Cornell University

Grace Period

Some think a scant three-minute window stood
between escape and death, just time enough
to save them all, until the window shut.
As flames exploded from the bins, Samuel
Bernstein vainly tried to put them out
with pails of water, useless like the hoses

in the stairwells, limp for lack of pressure.
On the eighth floor, Dinah Lipshitz counted
piecework. She had a telephone at hand,
but in her panic chose a new device,
a *tele-autograph*, to "text" her warning
to the office on the tenth. She scrawled out

"Fire" but the word did not appear
upstairs, and so she waited…when she phoned,
Mary Alter, subbing at the switchboard
and doing other work, was slow to answer.
When she did pick up she heard the screams
of "fire." Mary dropped the phone to tell

the bosses, while Dinah dangled on the line.
As each second passed, more lives were doomed.
She had no way to warn the floor between.
A message from the eight floor to the ninth
had to be connected by the switchboard
on the tenth, which was now abandoned.

The paper patterns, strung on wires down
the rows between machines, ignited like
a fuse and fire shot across the room,
while upstairs happy girls were singing songs.
The fragile factory had no tolerance
for error. The time of grace had come and gone.

Joseph Zito

Kheel Center, Cornell University

The Elevator Boy

They don't go sideways, only up and down,
so why is it so slow to reach us then?
Heedless of the need, the cables seemed
to slip like they were winding slack or made
of rubber, stretching time. *The week is over.*
Don't they know that dinner's on the table?

Joseph Zito, the "elevator boy,"
though twenty-seven, would have been a "boy"
forever on this job. He and Gaspar
waited in the lobby to be summoned
by the bells to bring down passengers.
It was quitting time, tomorrow Sunday.

The elevators were designed for twelve
to fifteen people. Cables ran up through
the middle, and had mesh on top. The shaft
was open overhead and disappeared
in darkness. When the bells began to ring
they sounded desperate, he could sense the fear.

He stopped at all three floors. He saw the flames,
the panicked workers on the window ledges,
how they clawed their way, wild-eyed,
on the overcrowded cars, and how some jumped
down the empty shaft and crashed on top
of other passengers. Joseph returned

again and again, while above, the fire
rained debris that streaked like fireworks.
With each trip down, his life was saved as well
but, going up into the flames alone,
unsure of coming down, made him a hero.
The man had saved one hundred and fifty lives.

After ten or so trips, the rails buckled
from the heat and stalled the elevators,
and Zito was arrested by the police.
A material witness, they said. When the DA
arrived at the scene and heard the story and saw
the horror, he had him released.

"Love Amid the Flames"

William Gunn Shepherd
Milwaukee Journal, March 27, 1911

By chance, William Shepherd, a reporter
for United Press, was in the park
and saw the smoke rise and the growing crowd.
He raced to the scene and phoned in the story
as it happened, to a young Roy Howard
who telegraphed it to the nation's papers.

Amid the flames, he saw a young man help
a girl climb out the window, hold her from
the ledge, then calmly let her go. She dropped
to the pavement, a deliberate act,
repeated with a second and a third,
unresisting, and all with courtesy,

as though he held an open door for them,
their gallant usher to eternity.
Behind, a dreadful death awaited them,
and calmly, they accepted one last act
of mercy, his brave, terrible chivalry.
The fire ladders arrived, but failed to reach.

One girl at the window stood as flames
surrounded her, removed her hat and sailed
it grandly on the air, then shook her purse
and threw down all her money, one last gift
to those who watched her from the street below.
She jumped, following the bills and coins.

The last girl appeared, his sweetheart, some say.
She threw her arms around the young man's neck,
and kissed him good-bye. He then held her out
in space and let her go, and followed her.
His coat fluttered upward, the air filled
his trousers. He wore a hat, tan shoes, and socks.

Roy Howard founded the Scripps-Howard newspaper syndicate.

Alternate Realities

Let's say the man who jumped was Jacob Klein,
and say the girl was not his sweetheart, just
one of scores of girls he knew by sight.
Let's say on that burning sill, it was
a first and only kiss that bought the moment
which they lavished on each other's face,
devoid of blemish, cant, reserve, each stripped
of posture, emptied, unashamed.
Not just *shalom*, the kiss, distilled, contained
the lifetime's sum of love they'd never live;
and then, as heaven teetered on the ledge,
he let her go, and empty-handed, followed.
Let's say the girl was Daisy Fitze. Because
we'll never know, let's make her bright and brave.

Daisy Lopez Fitze was from Jamaica. She and Bertha Greb were the only two victims identified on their death certificates as being Protestant. Of the remaining victims, about two-thirds were Eastern European Jews, and one-third Italian Roman Catholics. Both Daisy and Bertha are listed as having leaped to their deaths.

Kheel Center, Cornell University

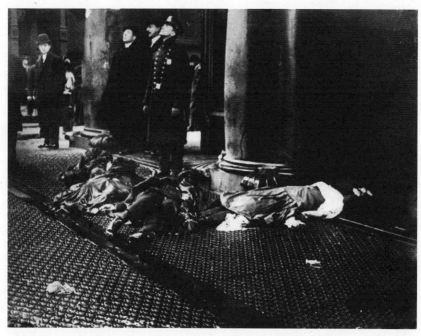

The victims' bodies were brought across the street as spectators watched helplessly.

Kheel Center, Cornell University
Photographer: Brown Brothers, March 25, 1911

Extinguished

When the rescue workers found me they must
have thought that I was dead, because they laid
me on the sidewalk with the other bodies.

Sarah Friedman Dworetz

The water from the fire hoses slapped
the walls, then gushed back like a waterfall
and drenched the heap of corpses on the sidewalk.
The blood that stained the twisted hoses drained
in rivulets between the cobblestones
to ultimately empty in the sea.

Not one survived the fall. Doctors and interns
from New York Hospital treated the injured
amid the chaos. Men who handled the dead
had to cover their ears to shut out the screams.
When it was safe the bodies were laid in rows
across the street, then covered and tagged.

By then the streets were clogged with thousands. Friends
and relatives, frantic with fear, pleaded
for news about their loved ones. Policemen formed
a line the mob soon overwhelmed. They swung
their billy clubs to drive them back. The surge
broke through the line again. At last, the crowd

was spent; despair and order were restored.
The police began to lower bodies down
the building's face, while other officers
were stationed at the windows, there to keep
the wrapped remains from banging on the walls.
Dozens of hearses began to arrive to carry

their cargo. People followed them on foot
with outstretched arms, calling names, and begged
to learn if loved ones were among the dead.
The Mercer Street Precinct was mobbed. It was dark
by then. The crowd was redirected north
two miles to the morgue at Misery Lane.

Viewing bodies at Misery Lane. Friends and relatives or curiosity seekers?

Kheel Center, Cornell University

Misery Lane

The city morgue, not up to task, diverted
wagons to the pier at Twenty-Sixth Street
and the river. The cavernous shed they called
"Misery Lane" had served some seven years
before as temporary morgue for a thousand
who died in the *General Slocum* disaster.

The Municipal Lodging House, a block away,
conscripted able residents to aid
the police. These so-called derelicts were called
to lay the bodies out in wooden coffins.
They placed them head-to-head in two long rows
and worked all night. They held the swaying lamps

above the bodies, helping relatives
identify them in the ghastly light.
Come closer, please, more light! I can't be sure.
They stood by, held up relatives who fainted,
they comforted as best they could, and swabbed
the floors with disinfectant, loaded hearses.

The men who worked anonymously knew
of hopelessness and loss, were not so far
removed from those they served, alive or dead.
One hopes they briefly rose above themselves,
felt useful with no need for thanks. They soon
enough returned to their reality.

The police had gathered up possessions left
behind by victims and brought them to the pier.
By midnight two long lines, estimated
in the thousands, began to form; people
shuffled down the rows of open coffins
with hope and dread and cruel uncertainty.

*On June 15, 1904, 1,021 lives were lost, when the excursion steamer
General Slocum burned and sank in the East River.*

Sunday Outing

a rag, a bone, and a hank of hair
                        Rudyard Kipling

The crowd grew coarse. By Sunday morning thieves
and ghouls, the idle curious, began
to gather. Now the line stretched out of sight
while those who needed information stood
their turn along with frock-coated men
on an outing with their giggling girlfriends.

The rich grew huffy in their limousines
when turned away, and busy policemen rousted
known pickpockets who schemed to work the line
and rob the bodies. Peddlers pushed cheap rings
in matchboxes, shouting "Souvenirs,
a ring from the finger of a dead girl!"

The police had seen enough and culled the crowd
of gawkers. Minutes later thousands turned
to hundreds. With the sensitivity
of nurses from the Charities Department,
the task to identify and claim
the dead proceeded inside, one by one.

For many, all that made them what they were
had burned away, reduced to rags and ash.
A braid of hair was all the Rosens had
to claim their mother, one gold tooth helped find
Mary Leventhal. And Kate Leone?
An anguished guess by Uncle Dominick.

At coffin 34 Rosie Soloman
hesitated; she thought she recognized
a signet ring. *Was there a pocket watch?*
There was. Inside, her photograph stared back
at her. She fainted. It was Joseph Wilson,
her fiancé. They planned to wed in June.

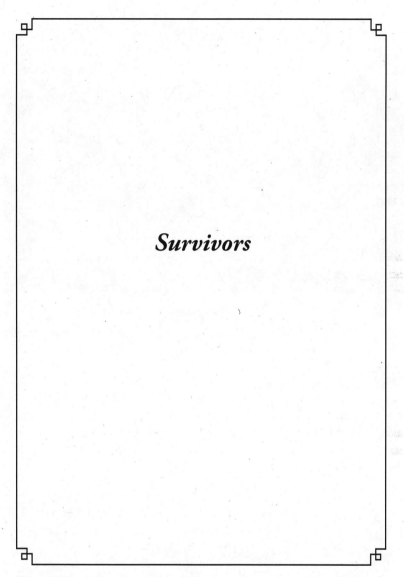

Survivors

The survivors' accounts are based on transcripts and tape recordings made by Leon Stein while doing research for his book The Triangle Fire. The witnesses were in their sixties and seventies at the time.

Thousands lined the route of the funeral procession.

Kheel Center, Cornell University

Lamentation

Three days later, Wednesday evening, thousands
held a packed memorial for victims
organized by Local 25.
The Grand Central Palace overflowed
with grieving friends and relatives in black.
Some had broken shivah to attend.

When Mayor Gaynor's name was mentioned jeers
erupted. Gaynor was perceived a flunky
of the rich and for the status quo,
and with their comrades' bloodstains on his hands:
"Bomb City Hall!" "Blow up the place!" The crowd
was in a mood to riot. To settle them down

the chairman gaveled for order—and a pause
for silent prayer in honor of the dead.
They settled in a hush. A woman sobbed,
then someone screamed, the keening rang across
the hall. The tension snapped and people sprang
up to their feet. Some tore their clothes in a kind

of "elemental and ecstatic mourning."
Grand Central Palace split with a single shriek
of mass despair. Survivors, who were seated
on the stage, called out names of loved
ones lost, and women fainted to the floor.
Captain O'Conner had sixty extra men

on duty to calm the crowd. They carried women
from the hall to save them being trampled.
Emergency wagons were called. With calm restored,
the crowd, now purged of its hysteria,
had settled down, and everyone listened
in sorrow and silence to the rest of the speakers.

Shivah, in Judaism: a week-long mourning period.

The funeral procession headed north on Fifth Avenue. The Washington Arch is in the background.

Library of Congress

The Wave

All week the funeral processions crossed
each other on the Eastside's grid of streets
and avenues, sometimes mingling mourners
with the wrong cortège. Union officials
organized two public funerals
for seven victims unidentified.

New York City owned a plot in Brooklyn's
Cemetery of the Evergreens,
and plans were made for burial after
the funeral processions, set for Wednesday
afternoon, one month after the fire.
On the day, low swollen clouds dragged

themselves across the building tops and spilled
a thick, black rain that drenched the mourners. Crowds
were gathered north and south of Washington Square,
with one asembled south around Canal,
the other north at Twenty-Second Street.
They planned to come together at the park.

One hundred and twenty-five thousand people
slogged through rain, four hundred thousand lined
the route, a half-million musty coats,
a million leaky shoes. Washington Square
was quilted with umbrella tops that let
the rain drip down people's necks, and ruin hats.

A flower-filled hearse was drawn by horses past
the rows of tenements. The usual
cacophony of languages fell mute
as it approached, and as it passed them by,
again the wailing. Their handkerchiefs fluttered
and then subsided like a passing wave.

Relief

At last, its conscience rattled, New York rose
to help the victims' families. The next
day, Sunday, Mayor Gaynor asked for funds
on their behalf. By ten o'clock on Monday
morning, office space was opened up,
given by a life insurance company,

and squads of visitors made rounds to homes
of the bereaved with five thousand dollars
in hand for distribution, and by Tuesday
the garment workers organized their own
assistance program. Funds came pouring in
from every source and every social class.

The Red Cross and Salvation Army each
raised funds along with other benefit
events: theatrical performances,
the symphony, the opera, vaudeville
and plays, and prizefights. George M. Cohan sang
and Al Jolson emceed shows to help.

Of course, there were the *schnorrers*, con men out
to scam the families, the kind who sold
the greenhorns subway tickets for a trip
to Iowa, yet charity prevailed,
and thousands were distributed to help
the proudly self-reliant families.

This one thing at least went right; the aid
was fast, efficient, unencumbered by
bureaucracy, was fair and generous,
funerals were paid for, as well as passage
that brought relatives from Europe; some
were helped to start a business of their own.

Voices

For years some never spoke about the fire,
some still panicked at the sound of bells,
the smell of smoke, sirens, closed-in rooms.
Others comforted themselves with stories,
the edges blurred, grown smoother with each telling.
Some needed to be coaxed, the pain so deep.

Their worst memories were buried, sealed
away like artifacts in time capsules
which kept them sane enough to live their lives.
Once cracked, the details spilled like beans across
linoleum, the once unspeakable
was spoken of, the terror of the day.

Their voices are the voices of the dead.
Alike in hope and promise, close in age,
their lives also turned on chance, on fear
or lack of fear of heights, turning left
instead of right, leaving early; all
alike except their final agony.

Life is unfair we say, but worse, we fear
it's random. Or we say, *We live by grace*,
until it's yanked out from beneath our feet,
in which case we repeat, *Life is unfair*,
as would the grandmother of the two
dead girls, as would Rose Hauser's landlady.

Most survived the day because of luck,
and then the years because of youth, support
of friends and family. They knew hard lives
were lived on peaks of joy, a favorite song,
a girlfriend's laugh, a green woolen skirt,
a hat with feathers that was never bought.

Homecoming

I had a broken arm and leg, and friction
burns from sliding down the cable.
I didn't want to go to the hospital,
I was only afraid of the shock to my mother.

Sarah Friedman Dworetz

As much explosion as a fire, most
were dead in minutes. Flames were spread so fast
that dozens jumped like skydivers spilling
from the windows. Their skirts and petticoats,
unlike parachutes to land them softly,
streamed and never caught the air to billow.

The wounded were attended to, the shocked
were left to wander home or gratefully
accept the help of strangers, telling us
a nice man took us home…or…gave us carfare…
or…*let me wear his coat,* and Rose, God knows,
met her girlfriend after work to shop.

They should have been in sunlight in the park
instead, laughing, flirting, but worked six days
a week and gave their pay to help support
their families who held them tightly. Mobs
and murder, pogroms in the Old Country,
these fears persisted in their parents' lives.

In turn, their daughters were afraid the news
might throw them into panic. One escaped
the hospital, because her mother was sick.
My God, one said, *I hope they don't find out.*
Not everyone was welcomed home. Until
the truth was known, some were treated harshly.

Ethel Monick Feigen

There were rumors women died frozen stiff
at their machines. I only know the flames
rushed in so fast some had no chance. It burst
in through the windows from the floor below.
The Greene Street elevator cable broke,
and the door on the Washington Place side was locked.

I heard them laughing in the dressing room
and realize now they were hysterical
and must have known they were about to die.
I went to the window to jump, but when I looked down
I felt ashamed about how I would look.
A crowd pushed me on an elevator.

When I got to the street, I felt like I
was in a bad dream. I scratched at my face
and tore my hair to wake me up. A man
from the *Journal* took me to the subway.
It was my first subway ride, because
I used to take the Third Avenue El.

My father would give me a nickel to go to work,
a nickel to come home, and one for lunch.
Because of the fire I got home late, exhausted.
I was dirty and I smelled from smoke.
My father gave me a licking. I hollered, "But, Pa,"
while my mother stood in the corner and shivered.

He wouldn't listen and called me a *bummike*,
a slut, and I had to go to bed.
I was half unconscious, half asleep.
I guess while I was still in bed they learned
the truth, because when I woke up, they were
huddled all around and kissing me.

Rose Hauser Glantz

I used to sing in the shop. That day the girls
insisted that I sing, *Every Little
Movement Has a Meaning of Its Own.*
The fire burned below us as I did
my little number in the dressing room,
then smoke began to billow up the stairs.

The door was locked, but I was too afraid
to jump. The back staircase door was open,
so I pulled my muff up over my head
and stumbled through the flames. I was numb
but then remembered that I had to meet
my girlfriend after work. She didn't know

about the fire, and she scolded me
for being late. We never bought that hat.
I didn't tell my mother. When she learned
the truth about what happened, she collapsed.
It was then that I began to cry
and must have cried for hours on my bed.

Our landlady had an only daughter
I was friendly with, who worked with me,
and when the mother learned that I was saved,
she came into our house yelling in grief,
and screamed, why had I not saved her daughter.
The poor woman seemed to lose her mind.

Long after, I was still afraid to walk
along her block or neighborhood, afraid
we'd meet. At night I dreamed of falling out
the window. I would scream and wake the house.
I remember hollering, "Momma,
Momma, I just jumped out the window."

Rose Cohen Indursky

The greenhorns had a saying that I kept
repeating, "In America they don't
let you burn." I ran for the elevator.
The door was open, but the driver went
to get the bosses on the floor above,
all the time my hair was smoldering.

That's when I ran upstairs and saw a man
collecting papers, shouting out for me
to run up to the roof. Who knew the floor
above me was the roof, or that there was
a fire escape? It was a lucky thing,
because it fell apart, and people died.

That bookkeeper saved my life. While on
the roof we tried to hold a girl who tore
herself away. She ran downstairs to find
her sister, and was lost. One youngster lived
who wrapped a roll of white goods all around
her body. I helped her to slap out the flames.

I lived with my uncle and aunt. When I got home
I fell across my bed and cried. They yelled
at me for acting like an animal.
I told them I was in a fire, but they
were old. I couldn't make them understand.

My mother was sick and lived in Białystok.
I was worried she would learn what happened.
A long time afterward I still had nightmares
and shook in my sleep. I was too afraid to pick up
my pay and when I did, that's when I learned
who lived, who died. I was sixteen at the time.

Mary Domsky Abrams

There was a cheerful feeling on the floor
that day. One girl was engaged the night
before. Her name was Esther and she wore
a diamond ring. She was lively and pretty,
her joy was contagious and we felt content
as we sewed and joked, oblivious of time.

She made us all so happy. She returned
to her machine from the dressing room
after the bell and perished in the flames.
She had a younger brother, Max. Esther
got him his job at the company.
He was in the fire but survived.

Across from me a boy sat, Jacob Klein.
He was so handsome and intelligent
the girls would raise their eyes and gaze at him.
He planned to start a drug store. During lunch
he went to the bank, and when he came back late,
we laughed and wished him luck. He also died.

One day, I visited a gnarled and sad
old grandmother. She had two girls who died.
She knew me. "You're an atheist," she cried,
"and God didn't punish you? My girls
were pious girls, so it must be better
to be like you and not serve God. Is this just?"

She wailed and lifted up her hands to heaven.
The woman broke into tears; we tried, but she
was unconsolable. I also went
to visit Esther's folks. The father gave thanks
his son survived. The night before she died,
Esther sang *I Didn't Come to Say Good-bye*.

Ida Nelson Kornweiser

I must have been a child, fourteen, say,
when they used to shove me in the toilet
to hide from the inspector. The day before
the fire I bought a brand new hat and left
it in the dressing room. I had my pay
in hand, then heard someone shouting, "Fire!"

I looked across the shop, and everything
was burning. So I left the hat and clutched
my pay, and I remember that I raised
my skirt and stuffed the money in my stocking,
then found a roll of cloth, white lawn I think,
and wrapped it all around my body.

With just my face exposed, I ran ahead,
right through the flames into the stairway hall.
The lawn caught fire as I ran upstairs.
I peeled it off me, twisting as I ran
while it burned, and by the time I reached
the roof, most of it was left in ashes,

but I was still on fire. A woman helped
me beat the flames out. I got minor burns.
We were saved by students next to us
from NYU who laid some boards across
one building to the other, but I never
panicked. I always knew what I was doing.

They took me to St. Vincent's Hospital
and made a bed for me, but I sneaked out
because my mother was sick. I ran home.
I was afraid of what might happen to her.
If I knew what a tragedy it was,
I wouldn't have taken the time to hide my pay.

Celia Walker Friedman

We came to America when I
was five years old. Because I had no Yiddish
accent they all took me for a Yankee.
My job was to check the waists to make sure
they were properly sewn. From where I sat
I saw all the way across the shop.

The aisles were narrow and cluttered with chairs,
and when the flames came shooting up outside
the windows, I was scared. People began
to scream and some started to fall in the flames.
The stairway door was blocked by stacks of crates.
We hollered for the elevator man,

and when he came the girls squeezed on ahead
of me, so I missed the elevator
and the next one, too. The crowd forced me
from behind into the open shaft.
Maybe it was panic, maybe instinct,
I jumped into the dark and grabbed the cable.

The next thing I knew, I opened my eyes
and looked into the face of a priest and a nun.
My head was injured and my arm was broken.
I was saved by sliding down the cable.
It left me with a scar down the middle
of my body from the friction of the fall.

The nurses said how smart I was to use
my muff to save my hands. I wasn't smart.
The word is vanity. I saved for weeks
to buy myself a brand new muff, and fire
or no fire, I held on to that muff
even while I jumped to save my life.

Josephine Nicolosi

They're all dead, Momma

Sal Marchesi liked to kid around,
so when he said, "There's a fire," I thought
he was joking. It started small, like a match,
below a cutting table. Sal threw a pail
of water on it, poof, it just exploded.
Flames shot up, and soon were everywhere.

I ran to the window but decided
not to jump. I didn't have the nerve.
Some girls believed the firemen would catch
them in the nets they held out on the sidewalk.
One girl, Vicenza Benanti, was engaged
to my cousin Frank. She had the nerve.

The machinist, Leo Brown, had found
a key. I grabbed him from the back, and he
unlocked the door, I followed him downstairs.
The first thing we saw were the girls lying
on the sidewalk. My girlfriend went to help,
and she was killed by a falling girl.

I was hurt and staggered home, right down
the middle of the street. My father was getting
a shave in the barbershop. Someone told him
"Your daughter is coming. She's all covered in blood."
He ran from the shop, lathered, towels flying
and bellowed, "Who did it?" and shook me by the shoulders.

The whole block could hear him shout, "Who? I'll kill him!"
and windows opened, including my mother's. She came
down screaming and crossing herself. My father thought
a boyfriend slashed me. While my mother cried,
I fell into her arms and sobbed, "*Momma,
tutti morti. Tutti morti, Momma.*"

Joseph Flecher

I was the office manager and worked
for Blanck and Harris maybe fifteen years.
On the tenth floor I had an office
and was handing out the pay. I heard
an awful noise, "fire, fire." Smoke
was coming up the elevator shaft.

I thought, "I must take care of myself. *C'est moi.*"
I ran to the roof. The roof of NYU
was six feet higher and I saw a wire
hanging down and thought I'd better climb.
Others followed, but the wire broke
and they fell down to Greene Street and were killed.

The next day the fire chief himself,
Edward Crocker, asked me to report.
I said "Mr. Fire Chief, may I ask
a favor of you? You will thank me later,"
and I asked him to exclude the press.
I told him the doors opened to the inside.

"Is it possible to open a door
when forty people push against it?" Also,
I said, "Mr. Crocker, I don't know
your system, your hose—excuse the expression—
only pissed to the fourth floor," and he says,
"Mr. Flecher, thank you for kicking out the press."

Oh, sure, there were strikes. We hired hoodlums
to take care of things, and their girlfriends,
you know, prostitutes. We had a captain
in the fifteenth precinct, our hundred-
dollar man. This is how we licked things.
We had protection from the police department.

Accused

Lesson

Delivered by Rabbi Stephen S. Wise on April 2, 1911 at a memorial meeting in the Metropolitan Opera House.

The lesson of the hour is that while
property is good, life is better,
that while possessions are valuable,
life is priceless. The meaning of the hour
is that the life of the lowliest
worker in the nation is sacred
and inviolable, and, if that sacred
human right be violated, we shall
stand adjudged and condemned before
the tribunal of God and of history.

Max Hochfield

My father, when he came here, loved this country
because he loved fish and he bought fish here
very cheap. Well anyway, he thought
to be an operator was the best
trade in the world. My sister wanted me
to be a carpenter, a plumber, a man's job,

but my father told her she should take me
to the Triangle. On Sunday night
they made her an engagement party, so
on Monday we missed work. Tuesday, they gave us
machines on the ninth floor, instead of the eighth.
Most people on the eighth got out alive.

So, if I was superstitious I would say,
if my sister wouldn't have this party
she might be alive today. They locked the door,
because each night the girls would open up
their pocketbooks to show they didn't steal
some lace or trimmings. I went back for her,

but the firemen, they wouldn't let me.
She was one of the strikers in nineteen-nine.
Her name was Esther and she burned to death.
I wanted to take my revenge on the firm.
I thought of an idea. I would buy
a gun and shoot these guys when the bosses

gave out back pay. But I was penniless,
and needed my pay in order to buy the gun.
I went to Local 25 to borrow
the money, and I was told, "Don't do it. Forget it."
Still, if I had the money, and knew where to buy
a gun, maybe I would have gone through with it.

Chain of Guilt

Guilty! A man, a cutter likely, flipped
a match, or cigarette into a bin
of scraps despite the posted signs that read
"No Smoking." Did he know what he had done?
Through arrogance or mindlessness, the act
was stupid, with unspeakable results.

The architects and Joseph Asch, guilty
of cutting corners, Harris and Blanck, for crowded
spaces, disregard of safety rules,
and lack of common sense in locking doors.
They never took responsibility
or changed, were never haunted by the dead.

The girls resented purses being searched,
the lack of trust, the loss of privacy.
At ninety-three, Pauline Pepe said,
"No one made a whole blouse. That one was tucking,
this one made sleeves, they were just young girls,
they wouldn't bother to steal."

But Harris didn't think so, that's why he locked
the doors. Employees stole, he testified
in court. He had caught them with the goods,
but when cross-examined he admitted
the total value of the pilfered goods
through the years was less than thirty dollars.

Moral Hazard

A flood? How do you arrange a flood?

Max Blanck had two daughters, Henrietta
and Mildred, who were waiting in the office
on the tenth floor, hoping to go shopping
with their father. During the fire they fled across
the roof to NYU, frightened but safe.
Arson was not suspected in the case.

Garment makers fretted over excess
inventory, trade was seasonal
and fashions fickle. When Paris sniffed at feathers
on women's hats, three feather factories burned
in New York City. When the French decreed
the simple skirt, three embroidery

and braid factories were incinerated.
In 1911, when Paris favored
the one-piece dress, with shirtwaists soon passé,
a rash of shirtwaist factory fires swept
the city because insurance could be bought
above the value of the goods insured,

and safe and unsafe factories paid the same.
There were no incentives for safety, like sprinklers,
quite the opposite, the practice bred
negligence and fraud. In a system that stank,
the Triangle was known as a "rotten" risk
but the owners found a silver lining.

Of the money they collected from
the fire, sixty-four thousand dollars
was for goods they could not document.
A clear profit that averaged four-hundred-
and-forty dollars per life lost in the fire.
Worker safety was simply not a factor.

Status Quo

Progressive movements grew and fought against
the bureaucrats, the courts, and politicians
who sided with the owners, who believed
there was no right to strike. The status quo
was God's intended order. Obstacles
to commerce were discouraged by the law.

Other sweatshops shared the guilt, as did
the businessmen whose moral values failed
to transfer to society at large.
Equality, social justice, kindness?
Religious teachings? Well and good inside
the home, but not inside the factory.

They lost their way, forgot their decency,
succumbed to moral fragmentation, let
themselves degrade their workers like they were
commodities. Oppress Rose Glantz by day,
at night go home to kiss the wife and kids
and pet the dog; a culpable blindness.

The safety laws were weak and unenforced,
and warnings from concerned departments went
unheeded. People in America
were passive to the suffering that lay
behind their clothes; for all they knew, or cared,
their clothing might as well be made in China.

The calls for higher wages prompted threats
by businesses to leave the city, to search
for cheaper labor. In the years to come,
as garment workers unionized themselves,
and their wages rose, and conditions improved,
the industry flourished, and so did New York City.

Max Steuer (sounds like lawyer)

At last, the public's conscience found its voice.
The calls for punishment forced bureaucrats
to duck inside a maze of regulations,
while politicians, from the governor
on down, jockeyed to divert the blame,
leaving Harris and Blanck to face a charge

of manslaughter in the first degree.
Just six days past the fire, facing jail,
the two sprang into action with a plan
to buff their public image, and began
a four-month ad campaign. They placed about
five-thousand-dollars worth of advertising.

The Catholic News and *New York Sun* declined,
along with others. The *New York Call* returned
their check, but not before they published it
and ran the story. The partners pled financial
hardship, yet Blanck and Harris found the cash
to hire New York's top defense attorney.

Max Steuer (sounds like lawyer) was like Blanck
and Harris. He was bright, resourceful, ruthless,
and another immigrant made good.
His legal fee, a fortune at the time,
was ten-thousand dollars each, upfront.
He came from the same tenements

and slums as did the witnesses. He spoke
their language, knew first-hand their lives and fears.
His early cases dealt with unpaid bills
and broken contracts. With the insights gained
he plied every intimate technique
he knew to his advantage at the trial.

Prayer

From a sermon by Reverend Dr. R.S. MacArthur,
delivered at Calvary Baptist Church, March 26, 1911.

Merciful God, teach employers of labor
the duties which they owe to those under
their care in the proper construction of factories,
in making proper exits and in all
other ways caring for the comforts
and especially the lives of those in their employ.

If the law has been violated,
may punishment be swift and sure and just
and speedily inflicted.

Indictment

[Blanck] offered me $1,000 to change
my testimony. He said to me "Come here you.
Why you say the door is locked?" I said to him,
"That is the truth." He said, "How much do you want?"

Josephine Nicolosi

When the grand jury was convened
to hear from witnesses, seven Italian
workers filed affidavits charging
Samuel Bernstein and machinist Leo Brown
with attempted witness tampering.
Already, sleazy tactics had begun.

The two, ejected from the building, faced
no punishment and nothing came of it,
except to warn how far Steuer would go
to save his clients' skins. Indictments were issued
the following day. The defendants endured
their first perp walk past crowds that screamed *Murder!*

The public's appetite for scandal, dulled
by summer, was re-whetted by the trial.
The story reappeared but never would
be front-page news again. The world moved on.
At last the partners stood before the court
to face the people's wrath. The curtain rose.

Acting for the people: District Attorneys
Charles Bostwick and Robert J. Rubin.
Despite Steuer's reputation, both
attorneys felt the People's case was strong.
The "twelve good men" were found and took their seats.
The trial lasted over Christmastime.

The DAs' task would be to set the scene
and call their witnesses to testify
a ninth floor door was locked illegally
and therefore caused the death of Margaret Schwartz,
in whose death was gathered up the deaths
of all who might have lived had it been open.

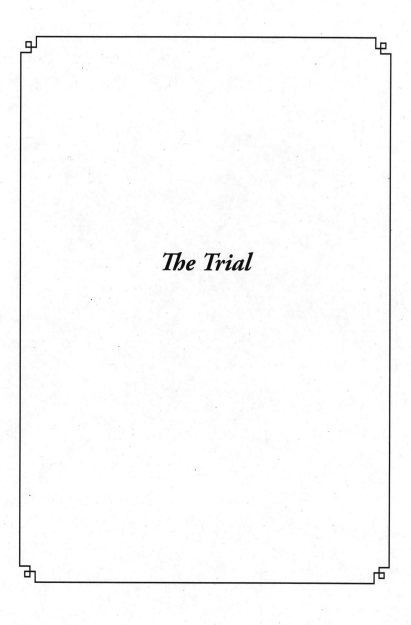

The Trial

TRIANGLE SHIRT WAIST MANUFACTURERS
LISTENING TO TESTIMONY AGAINST THEM

MAX BLANCK

ISAAC HARRIS

Kheel Center, Cornell University

In Court

The jurors all were *burghers*, solid men.
One was in shirts, another in cigars,
three salesmen, a buyer, clerk, an importer,
a secretary, painter, supervisor,
and one in real estate, all were white.
There were no women seated on the jury.

The witnesses were mostly girls who dressed
up in their Sunday best. They stood in awe
before the court, heads bowed, speaking low
in broken English, the translations barely
helped, while others gave off sparks and stood
their ground like the picketers on strike.

He tried to trick me when I testified,
and handed me a map and asked me where
the doors and tables were, but he couldn't,
because I told him "Turn the map around,
it's upside down!" and he replied, "You sure
do like to argue, don't you, little girl?"

Ethel Monick, age 16

Defense attorney Steuer summoned half
the witnesses the prosecution did,
and like the jury, all white-collar men.
The state called workers who were at the scene,
but under Steuer's cross-examination
most were easily intimidated.

Confused, and sounding unreliable,
they testified the door was locked. They pushed
and pulled and clawed, but it failed to open.
The salesmen and the office workers used
the stairs at will during the day, and swore
that when they used the door it wasn't locked.

Anna Gullo Pidone

I paid the people on the ninth-floor first,
then rang the bell to quit at four forty-five,
just like every Saturday, except
the eighth floor was burning at the time.
We were completely unaware until
someone in the dressing room yelled "Fire."

My sister worked with me. I kept crying
as I looked for her and couldn't find her.
The front door was locked, so I ran to the windows.
I looked down and made the sign of the cross
but I didn't have the courage to jump.
Because I worked there as a forelady

I knew about the staircase in the back.
I had my fur coat, a hat with two
feathers, and a green woolen skirt.
I pulled them over my head, and I ran down
as wind blew up the staircase in my face.
That night we found my sister at the morgue.

I testified for more than two hours.
The lawyer kept trying to catch me. Once in a while
he asked, "How many times did you open the door?"
I yelled back at him, "I never could open it,
it was always locked." Later he asked me again,
I screamed, "I couldn't open it at all."

Harris and Blanck were very nice to me,
but I lost my sister in that fire
and a neighbor who I helped to get the job.
She had five children and she burned to death.
I sued them later, but I lost my case.
I know that door was locked.

In a separate case Pidone sued for $25,000.

Witness

When Kate Alterman was on the stand
she testified three times how she had seen
Margaret Schwartz perish. Steuer's probes
created doubt among the jurors, not
so much for inconsistencies, but that
her stories were uncomfortably the same.

Despite the differences in each account,
the implication was she had rehearsed
and memorized her testimony, worse,
she had been coached in how to testify.
The state's star witness had her impact blunted
and her integrity impugned.

I tried, pulled the handle in and out,
all ways and I couldn't open it...
and then (Margaret) tried...I saw her down
on her knees...and I noticed the trail of her dress
and the ends of her hair begin to burn.

Kate Alterman

When the case was handed to the jury,
the judge instructed that to convict they must find
the door was locked, that the defendants knew
the door was locked at the time, and this
directly caused the death of Margaret Schwartz,
who might have otherwise survived the fire.

Two days after Christmas the jury retired
at 2:55 p.m. It polled itself
three times. The first vote, eight to two, with two
abstentions, and the next was ten to two.
Two hours later the verdict was in.
The trial, which lasted twenty-one days, was done.

Verdict

The gavel fell, a clap of oak on oak
that ricocheted around the room, the crack
an auctioneer might make to close the bidding.
Manipulation of the law, money's
quiet power, the court as auction house,
the trial done, the verdict in—sold.

Later, juror Victor Steinman, the man
in shirts, declared, "I know I have not done
my duty toward the people...I believed
the door was locked," but could not convict,
he said, and still obey the judge's charge.
Max Steuer, Blanck and Harris won their case.

The importer, Houston Hierst proclaimed,
"My conscience is perfectly at rest,"
(one could say asleep). To him the fire
was an act of God Almighty. The type
of girls employed "were not intelligent
and therefore more susceptible to panic."

The partners stood and heard the verdict calmly.
Mrs. Blanck then threw her arms around
her husband's neck and wept as officers
surrounded them and rushed them out the back.
They were confronted by a mob that cried,
"Where is justice?" and once again, "Murder!"

In nineteen-thirteen, Blanck was charged again
for locking factory doors. His new shop housed
scores of workers, also on the ninth floor.
The judge found him guilty. He was fined
twenty dollars, and got a personal
apology for his inconvenience.

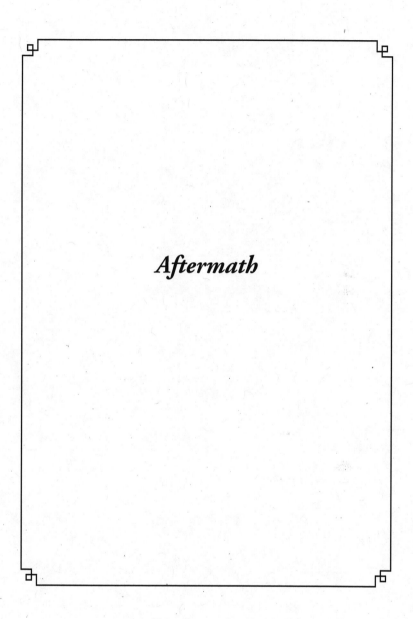

Aftermath

Awakening

In April, three days after thousands mourned
the fire's dead, a blast in Birmingham
tore through a coal mine, killing scores of men.
The men were black, and mostly convicts "leased"
to mining companies. The sympathy

was scant in Alabama, less across
the nation. Shortly, public interest waned,
like the Monongah mine in 1907,
where three hundred and sixty-seven died,
or two hundred and sixty-nine who died
in the Cherry Mine in Illinois.

Yet, this fire shocked America.
Not hidden underground in distant mines,
but white girls burned alive and crushed to death
upon the storied sidewalks of New York,
in public view, in front of citizens
who telegraphed the horror to the world.

Their moral torpor shattered, Anne Morgan,
J.P.'s daughter, who supported labor,
organized a rally at the Opera House.
It was packed with rare diversity.
They knew outrage was meaningless, until
transformed into action and reform.

In time, new safety laws were passed, and cursed
by business, ruled unconstitutional
in court, and passed again. Frances Perkins
called the fire, "the first day of the New Deal."
The body of law took thirty years to build,
and seventy more to be threatened again.

Frances Perkins, the first female cabinet member.

Sermon

From a sermon given by Reverend Dr. Charles S. Slattery
at Grace Church, Broadway and Eleventh Street, a few blocks
from the fire, March 26, 1911.

One of the facts that will confront the bereaved
is that the death of their loved ones was needless,
that someone was too eager to make money
out of human energy to provide proper safeguards
and protections. (New York should stop) and think
whether it was not allowing men
to go too madly and disastrously
and selfishly in pursuit of money.

And Here We Are

Pauline Pepe, at age 94.

I went to work against my mother's wish
because my friend said, "Come, we'll have a good time
working there." The girls were young and lots
of Jewish girls who were engaged. We ate
our lunch together. They were lovely girls.
Oh, we had lots of fun. I liked working there.

I did tucking, yards and yards of tucking,
for twelve dollars a week. Can you imagine?
Today, they must get a hundred. Who knew?
It was wonderful, we thought. You know,
I left my coat and pocketbook behind.
I never did collect that twelve dollars.

As soon as we heard "Fire," we ran out
the door, about a hundred-fifty maybe.
We screamed and tumbled down the narrow stairs.
They kept us in the lobby to be safe,
because the girls were dropping to the sidewalk.
We were crying. A nice man took us home.

When I got home I was all no coat,
no jacket, no nothing. "My God," I said,
"I hope they don't find out." They didn't know
what happened right away, but my sister,
she got so scared she got St. Vitus Dance.
My mother said, "Uh oh, something's wrong."

We were all so frightened, the Red Cross
gave us a vacation in the country.
They were wonderful, those people. After,
I did office work, then I got engaged
and I got married. That's all, and here we are,
seventy-five years later. Here we are.

More Locked Doors

I heard screams, and people yelling "Fire."
I tried to leave, but my supervisor
told me to get back to work. My sister
grabbed me by the arm. We went upstairs
to find a place where we could jump.
I was injured, but my sister died.

In 1993 Lampan Taptin's
sister died in Bangkok in a blaze
along with two hundred other workers
who made dolls of Santa Claus and Muppets
for children in America. The doors
were locked, the plant was cheaply built and crowded.

The site has since been leveled, scoured clean,
its very emptiness a monument,
but locals say the air still smells of smoke.
Two years before in North Carolina,
twenty-five died at Imperial Foods, who left
their footprints on the door that locked them in.

The story was repeated in Lahore,
Karachi, Bangladesh in 2012
with four hundred killed by fires due
to poor construction, greed, corruption, once
again, locked doors, each death preventable.
The shirtwaists sewn a hundred years ago

in Greenwich Village or in Bangladesh
today, depended on the same low pay,
thin margins, ruthless competition, threats
to move to cheaper countries, customers
who squeeze suppliers down to every cent
and won't invest it in a safer shop.

Eraclio Montanaro

I worked in a tailor shop. Since spring
was in the air, my friend and I quit early
and we took a walk. We saw people
running. We ran too and saw the girls.
The firemen held nets with bloody hands
made useless by a fall nine stories high.

The people around us were covered in blood.
My friend collapsed and cried like a woman,
as did other men who cried as well.
I got sick and couldn't look and ran home
to Henry Street. I don't remember how
I got there. All night long I lay awake.

In the morning I was restless, so I rode
the train uptown to Bronx Park. My chest,
it felt about to burst. Inside the park,
the Bronx River goes through the woods. I ran
the edges of that river all day long
like a wild animal or crazy man.

Years later I returned, I was old by then.
They call it now the Brown Building. I heard
the screams again and smelled the smoke. People
asked me why I stood there looking up.
I said, once there was a fire here.
I told my story, and they went on their way.

Epilogue

after Gregory Vlastos

We believe in truth and fairness or do not,
but cannot take up justice like we take
up golf, as an afternoon's diversion.

You are now a witness. If you turn
your face, the truth will grasp you by the neck
and bend you to confront these wrongs again.

Beyond the justice of the amateur,
a spirit in us makes us crave the truth
and warns that should commitment slip between

our fingers, fire, death, and sorrow wait.
You have seen it. There is no escape.
We wait and you must answer, yes or no.

Sources and Acknowledgments

Baker, Kevin. *Dreamland*. New York: HarperCollins 1999.

Cornell University. "Remembering: The 1911 Triangle Fire." Kheel Center for Labor-Management Documentation and Archives, School of Industrial Labor Relations, January 2011. www.irl.cornell.edu/trianglefire. This website exhibit presents original documents and secondary sources on the Triangle Fire, held by the Cornell University Library. The Cornell University Library Division of Rare and Manuscript Collections also contributed to the exhibit.

Kentop, Donald. "Frozen by Fire." *Drash: A Northwest Mosaic*. Volume VII. Seattle: Temple Beth Am, 2013.

— "Homecoming." *Here, There, and Everywhere*. Redmond, Washington: Redmond Association of the Spoken Word, 2013.

Llewelyn, Chris. *Fragments from the Fire. The Triangle Shirtwaist Company Fire of March 25, 1911: Poems*. New York: Viking Penguin, 1987.

Shepherd, William Gunn. "Love Amid the Flames." *Milwaukee Journal*, March 27, 1911. The poem is dawn from Shepherd's eyewitness account. He was the only professional journalist who witnessed the fire.

Stein, Leon. *The Triangle Fire*. Philadelphia: Lippencott, 1962. Reprinted by Cornell University Press, Ithaca, New York, in 2001. In addition to his valuable book, a particular debt of gratitude is owed to the memory of Leon Stein for collecting survivor interviews and audio recordings. Most were collected in the late 1950s when the survivors and Stein were elderly. The first-person accounts of survivors are drawn from Stein's transcripts. All were found online in the Kheel Center collection at Cornell University.

Von Drehle, David. *Triangle: the fire that changed America.* New York: Atlantic Monthly Press, 2003. Von Drehle provides essential historical context for understanding the story of the fire and deserves special acknowledgment for his research detailing the critical three minutes at the fire's start, during which time many lives might have been saved but for several critical breakdowns. The poem "Grace Period" is based on his account.

Donald Kentop was born in New York City. He is a graduate of New York University and Columbia with a masters degree in the teaching of history. His poetry has appeared in numerous journals. In 2004 Rose Alley Press published his chapbook *On Paper Wings*. He lives in Seattle with his wife Carol.